The Echinopsis Hybrids of Abbey Brook Cactus Nursery

*The results of 40 years' work
by Brian Fearn BSc MSc*

PLANT HERITAGE
National Council for the Conservation of Plants & Gardens
Patron: HRH The Prince of Wales

PLANT HERITAGE
NCCPG

Copyright © Brian Fearn 2009
The moral right of the author has been asserted.
ISBN: 978-0-9561698-0-8
All rights reserved. No part of this publication may be reproduced, stored in a retrieval system, or transmitted, in any form or by any means, without the prior permission in writing of the publisher, nor be otherwise circulated in any form of binding or cover other than that in which it is published and without a similar condition including this condition being imposed on the subsequent purchaser.
Designed and produced by Gilmour Print *www.gilmourprint.co.uk*
Published by Plant Heritage *www.plantheritage.com*

Contents

Foreword 4

Acknowledgements 5

Preface 6

Photography 8

Abbey Brook *Echinopsis* Hybrids
    The Results of 40 Years' Work 9
    Growing Instructions 12

The Check List 14
    The *Echinopsis* Hybrids 15
    The × *Trichoechinopsis* and × *Tricholobiviopsis* Hybrids 73

Analysis of Parentage 84

Plants used in the Production of
    the Abbey Brook *Echinopsis* Hybrids 85

Bibliography 96

Glossary 97

Index 99

Foreword

Perhaps it is unusual to start a book with two questions, but the answers to both are critical to this work:

1. Who has had the longest and greatest experience at quenching the UK demand for top quality seed-grown and propagated cacti?

2. Which terrestrial cacti above all others produce the largest flowers of the biggest range of colours in the greatest quantities?

Answers: Brian Fearn and *Echinopsis* hybrids.

I started growing succulents in the 1950s and I bought plants from all existing nurseries specialising in cacti. It is most pertinent that I still have almost all the plants acquired from Abbey Brook while none survive from other nurseries (now mostly disappeared).

Most growers of cacti feel real achievement and the pinnacle of joy when their plants flower. In the 1950s, most of my success was from Victorian *Echinopsis* hybrids that invariably had night-flowering white or pale pink petals and throats. Careful husbandry alongside the introduction of new material from the New World has meant that flowers of hybrids in every warm shade and combination of colours are now available.

I sometimes worry about a snobbery associated with genuine species with field data to the total shunning of cultivars. A small collection of *Echinopsis* hybrids draws immense interest even from those not already involved in the hobby. Stunning flowers of intense or subtle shades are likely to be produced throughout the warmer months in greenhouse or on windowsill and are a worthy addition to any plant collection.

Ray Stephenson

Acknowledgements

I wish to express my sincere appreciation to all those who have so generously given invaluable help, assistance and encouragement in the preparation of this booklet. In particular, I would like to thank Steven Thompson who is a member of my local East Midlands group of Plant Heritage.

I wish to thank Plant Heritage for its contribution to the funding of this booklet, for support over the last 12 years as a Collection Holder, and for the encouragement to increase my National Plant Collections to six, one of which has Scientific Status. The friendliness of my local group is much appreciated.

I also thank Graham Charles for kindly providing a photograph and for his consent to its publication here.

My wife Gill has been very supportive and very patient during the long hours of writing and rewriting, particularly when I wrestled with the word processor, as my typing skills are a little cumbersome. Without her encouragement this project would never have been possible.

Finally to my mother, Ruth Fearn, who died just short of her 95th birthday. She was a plantsperson all her life, and without her expertise and enthusiasm I would have accomplished very little. One of my latest × *Trichoechinopsis* hybrids has been named for her.

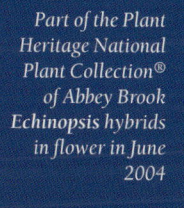

Part of the Plant Heritage National Plant Collection® of Abbey Brook Echinopsis hybrids in flower in June 2004

Preface

I acquired my first six cacti and succulent plants in 1947 and was promptly fascinated. I am still fascinated over 60 years later. I read botany at Sheffield University and graduated in 1959. Whilst at university, I turned a hobby into a business and founded Abbey Brook Cactus Nursery in 1956, naming it after the Abbey Brook which has its source on the nursery land. I have run the nursery full-time ever since leaving university. In 1976 we moved the nursery to the present site at Darley Dale, near Matlock, Derbyshire and in 2006 my wife Gill and I celebrated its golden anniversary.

In the late 1960s, I started hybridising *Echinopsis* and this booklet describes the results of my work in producing the Abbey Brook *Echinopsis* hybrids. I am not alone in working on the genus *Echinopsis*. There have been hybridisers in America, New Zealand, Germany, Holland, Japan and elsewhere. As far as I am aware, few have kept long term records of their crosses, so that the precise parentage of many hybrids is not known.

Echinopsis hybrids are grown mainly for their very large and beautiful flowers. I have sought to produce a wider range of flower colours and shapes together with other good attributes while keeping records of the crosses made. I have also produced hybrids with species of *Trichocereus*. The plants usually take about four years to flower from seed, although sometimes it can be less. Over the years 150,000 seedlings have been flowered and only just over 130 have been named. I am still, after 40 years, continually hybridising and selecting offspring.

My early *Echinopsis* hybrids are now grown all over the world, as they were distributed prior to 1988 by Abbey Brook Cactus Nursery. Since then, with the effects of the introduction of the CITES legislation (my hybrids are all covered by CITES, even though they have never seen a natural habitat), distribution has been restricted to the European Union.

It is not always possible to propagate straightforwardly all the hybrids vegetatively, as some of them never produce offsets. This means that years may elapse before sufficient plants are available for sale, which is reflected in the price. One can only be sure of a name by vegetative propagation, as seedlings are invariably different from their parents.

I have also long been interested in plant conservation. In the early years, as part of our conservation strategy, many plants were raised from wild collected seed. The resulting seedlings were distributed worldwide, making it unnecessary for anyone to deal in field collected plants. Unfortunately, this distribution of nursery propagated material has also become impossible due to the CITES legislation.

Over the years I have formed the Abbey Brook Cactus Nursery private collection. This comprises around 4500 species of cacti and succulents including many clonotypes and other material of conservation importance which I have made available through the nursery. The collection includes six Plant Heritage National Plant Collections® of which the Abbey Brook *Echinopsis* hybrids form one.

Photography

Except for Graham Charles' photograph of *Echinopsis calorubra*, all those in this booklet are my own work and copyright, but my photographic skills have been influenced by a number of people during the last 50 years. The late Horace Kennewell, a member of the Sheffield branch of the BCSS was an early influence in the 1950s. His branch slide shows were a step change from most others of the period. I made a mental note at the time of his careful use of blue for a background.

I learnt darkroom skills from Ted Barron and Glyn Woods in the Botany Department at Sheffield University where I developed and printed my own monochrome photographs. During this time I changed from using glass photographic plates in a quarter plate camera to an East German SLR Exa camera, and then moved on to an Exacta, which I used for the next 20 years.

Fifteen years ago I changed my system again to a Canon A1 with a 100mm Macro lens. At this time I was using two camera bodies, one loaded with slide film and the other with print film. Ten years ago I exchanged one of these bodies for a Canon T90 which was a more up to date system, in which all my lenses were still compatible. The photographs in this booklet have all been taken with this camera using Kodak 200 ASA print film. All the close-up photographs are taken using a tripod, delayed action shutter, and using aperture priority set at f22. I always use shaded natural light, never full sunlight, as the colours have a better balance. I was able to go digital with this system, getting a CD every time I had a print film developed.

I have now changed my photographic system yet again to a fully digital one. Unfortunately none of my Canon lenses, which have been so good in the past, fit my new Canon Eos 40D camera and I have had to invest in a new set. My slide projector is also redundant, as I am now using my laptop and a digital projector. This has made another problem as I have more than 10,000 photographic slides. These include photographs of my early *Echinopsis* hybrids as well as slides of plants in habitat in India, Mexico and America. I will now have to convert them all into digital format.

Abbey Brook Echinopsis Hybrids

The Results of 40 Years' Work

Darley Dale has long been favoured by plantsmen because of its aspect to the south west and favourable climate. It is sheltered from the north and east by a high ridge; this gives some protection from the worst of the winter weather. The first of many nurseries was founded here in the 1820s by James Smith. Many of these nurseries had a proud tradition of innovation and hybridisation. James Smith, for example, is probably best remembered for the production of *Erica* × *darleyensis* and *Campanula* 'Wheatley Blue'.

Sir Joseph Paxton, who was head gardener at Chatsworth, as well as becoming a Victorian entrepreneur, built Darley House for his family. It is only a stone's throw away from where I live and work at Abbey Brook. My work at Abbey Brook is in the same tradition, and many of my hybrids use the Darley prefix, as well as other local place names. A few are named for nursery staff and friends.

In the wild, *Echinopsis* and its relatives exhibit a wide range of flower colours, from pure white, yellow, to deep purple and red. The white flowered species are usually night flowering and often highly scented. The coloured flowered species are day flowering and not scented. The plants naturally occur over a vast geographical range, from Peru, Bolivia and Chile, to Argentina, including Paraguay, Uruguay, southern Brazil and also Ecuador.

The taxonomy of the group is not easy, as the delimitations of the various related genera overlap to the extent that a recently published work (Hunt 2006) has lumped them altogether into the single genus *Echinopsis*. This includes the following genera: *Acanthocalycium*, *Acantholobivia*, *Chamaecereus*, *Heliantho-cereus*, *Lobivia*, *Pseudolobivia*, *Setiechinopsis*, *Soehrensia* and *Trichocereus*.

Although no recent research has been done on these genera, they have been combined pending a better understanding of the group as a whole. However, as the group is so diverse, it seems to me that new research is likely to result in some names being changed yet again. In the interests of stability I think it would have been better to have left the revision of these genera until then.

I have always believed that hybridisation, or the lack of it, is often a good taxonomic indicator of relationships. Many *Echinopsis* seem to freely hybridise with *Pseudolobivia* and the Argentinean members of the genus *Trichocereus*. I have only managed to hybridise *Echinopsis* with a few *Lobivia* species but with *Acanthocalycium* not at all. I have no experience of hybridising with *Helianthocereus* as my plants have never flowered, although there are reports of success in California. Interestingly, some species of *Echinopsis* seem reluctant to hybridise, even with other species of *Echinopsis*, *E. leucantha* being such a species, although I have managed to produce some hybrid seed in 2006 for the first time.

Like all committed hybridisers, I have attempted to improve on nature by hybridising species and groups that never meet in the wild. Forty years ago, I only had a limited range of plants to work with but, as the years went by, different plants were acquired.

Hand pollination is always carefully done using sterile cotton buds. These are used once then discarded. Each pollinated flower is tagged with a number and the data is recorded. The system is flawed if this is not done immediately as the memory can play tricks.

During the last 30 years I have noticed that if I do not hand pollinate the flowers they do not produce seed pods. I now make no attempt to prevent flying insects getting into the glasshouse as those capable of pollinating *Echinopsis* flowers seem not to occur here, or prefer to pollinate other flowers.

The first Abbey Brook *Echinopsis* hybrids to be introduced were 'Buttercup' and 'Goldie' in 1976. During 1980, 120 different hybrid crosses were made, by which time I was using third generation hybrids as well as 30 different species of *Echinopsis* and *Lobivia*. A breakthrough came in 1984 with the flowering of my first multicoloured hybrid 'Darley Gold'. In 1986, successful hybrid crosses were being made which involved four different hybrids, each of which had complex parents. 'Brian's 6X' named in 2006 is one of these.

Since the start of the new millennium, many new hybrids have been named e.g. 'Streaky', 'Turkish Delight,' 'Gilly's Favourite', 'Golden Wedding' and 'Tango'. These are either completely different from previous hybrids, or great improvements on previous attempts. 'Golden Wedding ' is another of my × *Tricholobiviopsis* hybrids in the second generation, but it still does not surpass my original 'Chelsea Girl' of 1988, which according to Professor Gerhard Gröner was the first reported hybrid with yellow flowers in this group. He has also recently illustrated one of my yellow flowered × *Trichoechinopsis* hybrids in the German magazine *Garten praxis* (Gröner 2007).

'Derbyshire Sunset' *after pollination in 2007. The number 51 tags refer to a hybrid cross using 'Brian's Choice' as pollen donor. I will know the results of this cross in the year 2012. The plant has the typical spine formation and habit of* 'Ruffles'.

In 2006, I made 257 new hybrid crosses and in 2007 another 80. Many of these were fifth and sixth generation hybrids. Not all of these crosses set seed and there are many reasons for this, such as immature pollen, a receptor flower that was too old, or a complex hybrid that was not compatible with its pollen donor.

The germination percentage is very variable, sometimes nearly 100% is achieved, but with some samples of the more complex hybrids, 5% is a good result. There is occasionally total disappointment with zero germination, but this does not happen very often. I have also noticed that even when a good percentage germination occurs, some seedlings fail to develop. This is because they remain chlorotic (devoid of chlorophyll), and consequently die after two or three months.

Since the year 2000, seed of nearly 500 hybrid crosses has been sown. One hundred or two hundred seeds are usually sown of each seed sample, and with an estimated 50% germination this seed should produce another 50,000 seedlings. When past results are taken into consideration, this quantity of seed should yield another 50 or so plants which are worthy of a name, which works out to be about 1 in a thousand seedlings. It will not be before another ten years has passed, when I will be in my 80s, that the current crop of seedlings produced since the new millennium will have all flowered and been evaluated.

The selection process is quite long and laborious, but infinitely rewarding and satisfying. I am always looking forward to the next week or month, or even the next season, hoping for something new and different. Plants are usually at least four years old from seed before they start producing flowers. In a few hybrids, it may be a much longer wait. Flower production is just one of a range of characters which I am looking for. Other characters such as growth habit, solitary or clump forming, tall growing, the flower size and shape, number produced together and for how long, are all taken into consideration.

Apart from Bob Schick in America, as far as I am aware no one else has produced a comparable range of colour combinations. Certainly there is nothing else like 'Ruffles' which is now posted on the internet on Abbey Brook's home page at www.abbeybrookcacti.com. This is a new flower shape among *Echinopsis* hybrids as its ruffled petals conceal the throat of the flower.

Good plantsmen are remembered when they are living and working. Over the last 50 years I have been fortunate to have learnt from some of the best. I have known the following plantsmen, all now deceased, but I owe them a debt of gratitude for showing me how to grow plants successfully: Albert Baynes in Bradford, Stan Tomlinson in Sheffield, Fred Wass and Harry Watson in Nottingham, Mrs Coombes near Harlech, Dr H. W. de Boer in Holland, Fernando Riviere de Caralt of Pinya de Rosa at Blanes near Barcelona, D. Bouman in Naaldwijk, Holland and Robert Kuentz in Frejus, near Nice.

With the possible exception of Dr H. W. de Boer because he was intimately involved with the taxonomy of *Lithops* and *Conophytum*, all these plantsmen are now just names from the past.

Hybridists are a different breed, as they live on in the memory because the results of their labours and expertise remain with growers everywhere. Thomas Rivers, James Smith and George Russell for his lupins, were all horticultural hybridists and are remembered for the plants they produced. I hope that my name will be remembered as a plantsman, but above all for my work on *Echinopsis* hybrids. I know that my plants and hybrids have already given growers around the world much pleasure.

Growing Instructions

Echinopsis plants, like all cacti, make splendid subjects to grow in house, office or conservatory, as long as certain conditions are maintained.

Light
They must be grown in as light a position as possible. A greenhouse or conservatory is obviously the best place, but a sunny south or west-facing windowsill will be quite adequate.

Temperatures
Plants growing in greenhouse or conservatory conditions are often subjected to very high temperatures during sunny weather. Adequate ventilation must be provided otherwise the plants may become scorched. Cool dry conditions in winter are necessary for flowering. If you are growing your *Echinopsis* plants on the windowsill of a centrally heated room, then give them a winter break in an unheated spare bedroom, and they will reward you by flowering next spring. If you keep the plants perfectly dry in the winter months they can withstand cold, even frost!

Watering
Water the plants thoroughly once a week from the beginning of April to the end of September. During the winter months NO water should be given when cool conditions are being maintained. Plants kept in a centrally heated room continue to grow in winter and should be sparingly watered about once a month. However, they will not flower as well in the following year as plants that have been kept cool.

Feeding
During the growing season, apply low nitrogen, high potash feed every fortnight, such as Chempak Cactus Fertiliser or a tomato fertiliser.

Growing Medium
Grow the plants in a rich well-drained compost. A mixture of three parts houseplant compost to one part of coarse horticultural grit will be suitable. A top

dressing of sand or grit should be applied to the surface to prevent rotting around the base of the plant.

Pests
The main pest is mealy bug – these are small insects looking like miniature white woodlice which suck the sap and weaken and disfigure the plants. They also attack other houseplants such as saintpaulia and hoya. The use of a proprietary insecticide is recommended.

How to tell if your Echinopsis is Healthy
Healthy plants are usually deep green in colour under the spines, and are firm to the touch. Dead cacti are completely brown and shrunken in appearance (rather like a dead hedgehog). They are often soft, hollow or slimy and have no roots.

The Check List of Abbey Brook Echinopsis Hybrids

Introduction
In the following descriptions the hybrid's name is followed by its Accession Number and the year in which it was hybridised, introduced or named. The Seed Stock Number (where available) and parentage (where disclosed) are shown on the next line. The female parent (seed producer) is always given first, followed by the pollen donor.

Accession Numbers
When each accession is made to the Abbey Brook Cactus Nursery private collection it is given a sequential number with the prefix ABCN. The Abbey Brook *Echinopsis* hybrids are numbered within this sequence and their respective accession numbers are given in the Check List.

Seed Stock Numbers
When each batch of seed is harvested or received at Abbey Brook it is given a sequential Seed Stock Number with a letter prefix. Initially the cactus seed stock numbers began with the letter B and then C. From 1970, the CF prefix series (from Castcliffe Farm, our home in Derbyshire when the nursery was at Sheffield) was in use up to 1987 when the number 10,000 was reached. In the CF series alone an estimated 10 million seeds had been cleaned, sorted and counted. The prefix was then changed to AB which has been in use up to the present day. In all, the system has recorded the collection, naming, dating, cleaning and sorting of more than 25 million seeds of cacti in the last 50 years, the majority of which have been produced 'in house'.

Parentage
The practicalities of running a busy nursery mean that the pollen parent of some hybrids has not been recorded. This is shown in the Check List as " × collection", a term used by epiphyllum hybridists when the flowers are pollinated with whatever was in flower in their collection at the time, but not specifically noted.

Scope of the Check List
The following Abbey Brook *Echinopsis* hybrids are not included as no suitable photograph is available: 'Birthday Cake', 'Moonglow', 'Pineapple Crush', 'Pink Lipstick', 'Summer Dawn', 'Toreador' and × *Trichoechinopsis* 'Orange Beauty'. A further eleven hybrids have also been left out as they are no longer grown at Abbey Brook.

The Echinopsis Hybrids

'Abbey Brook' *ABCN 2189. 1976*

CF1634: *Echinopsis calorubra* × *E. calochlora* F$_1$. Deep salmon pink petals edged with violet, sepals brownish violet. Stigma and style yellow. Filaments crimson. Scented. This is a very early hybrid produced in 1976 at Castcliffe Farm.

'Alice in Wonderland' *ABCN 5598. 2005*

'Really Pretty' × 'Ruffles'.
Short-tubed flowers, petals white with magenta stripe, narrower at tip, broad at base. Petals changing to deep lavender pink as flower ages. Stigma and style yellow. Filaments yellow. This hybrid has clear links to 'Really Pretty', but the colour lines in the flower are more delicate, and the plant is different.

'Apple Blossom' *ABCN 4017. 1995*

Parents not disclosed.
Small pink and white flowers. Spineless plants. Outer petals with deeper pink midstripe. Stigma white, style green. Filaments white. Male sterile. Very floriferous. Although a relatively small flowered hybrid, it is worth growing because it produces so many flowers. The plant is also very attractive when not in flower, having rows of very close, white felted areoles.

'Apricot Fancy' *ABCN 2606. Not released*

CF6013: 'Darley Rose' × collection. Small pale apricot flowers with a hint of magenta on the petal edges. Darker orange midstripe. Slightly ruffled. Stigma and style yellow. Filaments orange. A very early hybrid dating from 1983.

'Ava' *ABCN 5609. 2005*

AB2851: 'Paramount Yellow' × collection. Hybridised in 1993.
Large wide-opening flowers. Petals salmon magenta with broad orange midstripe and ruffled edges. Sepals pale salmon with a greenish midline. Stigma and style yellow. Filaments orange.

There cannot be many plants that have been named after a motor car. AVA 562 which we have owned since 1983, is now part of the family. It is a 1938 Aston Martin 2 litre 2/4 sports which appeared on *BBC Gardeners' World* in 2006 during the Hampton Court Flower Show programme. This was recorded at Abbey Brook Cactus Nursery in Matlock prior to the show, with a follow up at Hampton Court on Press Day.

'Ballet Dancers' *ABCN 5086. Named in 2007. Not released*

Echinopsis leucorhodantha × *E. calorubra* F$_2$.
Fourteen flowers opened at the same time in 2007. Deep flesh pink flowers in cup and saucer form. Outer petals and sepals radiating, pinkish bronze. Stigma pale greenish. Style cream. Filaments white. Highly scented.

'Brian's 6X' *ABCN 5604. 2006*

'Lady Whitworth' ABCN 2592 × 'Neame's Apricot' ABCN 4371.
A complex hybrid involving 6 parents. Delicate pinkish salmon flowers suffused with lavender. Petals edged with lavender. Outer petals and sepals pale lavender with a prominent dark midline of greenish brown. Stigma yellow. Style green. Filaments deep orange. Scented.

'Brian's Choice' *ABCN 3278. 1975*

Echinopsis kermesina × *E. pereziensis* F_1.
Very large wide-opening flowers. Petals deep magenta purple. Sepals purple. Stigma white. Style magenta, Filaments purple. Highly scented.
This was my first really successful *Echinopsis* hybrid cross made in 1975. *Echinopsis kermesina* has long tubular flowers which barely open at the end and have little scent, whereas *E. pereziensis* has large white, wide open flowers which are highly scented. The resultant F_1 hybrid has huge wide open flowers. The plants are also extremely floriferous, the flowers being highly scented and a brilliant colour.

All the first generation plants are identical, which confirms that the two parents used were not of hybrid origin. It has never been released for sale because it rarely, if ever, produces offsets. I have not yet resorted to beheading the stock plants. They are still useful as parents, either as pollen donors, or as seed producers.

'Brooklands' *ABCN 2270. 1977. Not released*

CF2101: 'Buttermilk' × ('Green Gold' × *Echinopsis kermesina*).
Another early hybrid. Short-tubed flowers of deep golden yellow, each petal edged with orange. Outer petals and sepals with a median line of bronze. Flowers slightly ruffled. Stigma and style light yellow. Filaments golden yellow. Scented.

'Buff Beauty' *ABCN 2271. 1977. Not released*

CF4357: 'Darley Peach' × Johnson's unnamed hybrid.
Pale buff-salmon flowers with crimped petals. All petals sharply pointed. Stigma and style cream. Filaments orange. Scented. It has the same parentage as 'Crimson Glow' and 'Darley Lilac'.

'Buttercup' *ABCN 2207. 1976*

B241: *Echinopsis aurea* × 'Green Gold'.
Petals buttercup yellow, throat red. Sepals with a hint of magenta on the tips. Stigma, style and filaments yellow. One of the very first Abbey Brook hybrids produced in 1970. This hybrid is still very popular because it is easy to grow and flower. The prefix B is a very early seed stock number.

'Buttermilk' *ABCN 2253. 1978*

'Golden Dream' × *Echinopsis multiplex*
Creamy yellow petals with darker yellow midstripe. Stigma yellow, style green. Filaments cream. Highly scented. Like 'Buttercup', this is another of my very early hybrids between an American hybrid of unknown parentage and a long cultivated species.

'Cleopatra' *ABCN 3242. 1993*

'Lemonade' × collection

Very large wide-opening flowers. Petals creamy white with a very prominent and beautiful golden yellow midstripe. Sepals creamy bronze. Stigma and style creamy yellow. Filaments white. Highly scented.

This is an outstanding hybrid, well worth growing for its scent alone, doubly so because of its large yellow striped flowers. One of its parents 'Lemonade' is a very early hybrid but unfortunately I have no record of the pollen donor. A number of my other hybrids have also a yellow median stripe in the flower e.g. 'Darley Sunbeam' and 'Mystic Moon', but not as prominently as 'Cleopatra'.

'Crimson Glow' *ABCN 2168. 1978*

CF4357: 'Darley Peach' × Johnson's unnamed hybrid.
Short-tubed flowers. Petals deep crimson with rounded fimbriate margins. Median line of orange and yellow. Sepals pale yellowish orange. Stigma crimson. Style purple. Filaments crimson.

A strikingly beautiful hybrid which has inherited the crimson purple stigma of Johnson's unnamed hybrid. The fimbriate margin to the petals seems to be a rare character. This hybrid has not been released for sale as it is currently used for pollen and seed production.

'Crown of Gold' *ABCN 3700. 1985*

'Golden Dream' × collection

Huge flowers 20cm long 10cm in diameter. Petals deep golden yellow tinged with orange and magenta. Inner petals salmon orange, outer petals shading to golden yellow. All petals with an orange midstripe. Sepals light orange with a bronze midline. Stigma yellow. Style green. Filaments pink. Scented.

This hybrid was produced from flowers of 'Golden Dream' that had been pollinated with anything else that was in flower at the time. Unfortunately it is imprecise, as one has to speculate what the other parent might have been. 'Golden Dream' itself was probably produced in the same way, as most early American hybrids have unknown parents.

'Darley Ann' *ABCN 4079. 1995*

'Starlight' × 'Darley Pinwheel'
Large flowers of pale salmon pink with yellow orange midstripe, outer petals bronze yellow. Stigma white. Style green. Filaments cream. Scented.
An attractive hybrid with lots of narrow pointed petals.

'Darley Apricot' *ABCN 2250. 1985*

'Apricot Fancy' × collection
Very large flowers 10cm diameter and 18cm long. Pale apricot-orange flowers, outer petals tinged magenta with a deeper magenta midstripe. Stigma and style pale yellow. Filaments orange.

'Darley Beauty' *ABCN 2224. 1988*

'Ruffles' × collection

Large flowers with channelled and ruffled petals. Petals reddish crimson with orange midstripe and magenta edges. Petals shading to deep orange at the centre. Stigma yellow. Style green. Filaments white. Scented.

'Darley Hammerschmid' *ABCN 5901. 2006*

Echinopsis hammerschmidii × 'Brian's Choice'

Long-tubed magenta purple flowers. Sepals magenta bronze. Stigma yellow. Style magenta. Filaments deep magenta. Scented. Superb flowers.

A habitat collected plant of *Echinopsis hammerschmidii* was obtained in the late 1950s and has been propagated vegetatively ever since by Abbey Brook. It was used as a parent in the 1990s to produce this stunning hybrid. Please note this is the correct spelling of Hammerschmid without a 't'.

'Darley Gold' *ABCN 2166. 1984*

(*Echinopsis aurea* × 'Green Gold') × ('Green Gold' × *E. kermesina*)
Complex hybrid involving at least 4 parents. Large long-tubed flowers. Inner petals deep golden yellow. Outer petals shading to deep peach colour. Sepals lavender pink. Stigma and style cream. Filaments golden yellow shading to red at the centre. This makes the throat appear reddish. Scented.

This is the first of my bi-coloured hybrids, and the first really distinct hybrid produced after 15 years' work. 'Sunny Jim' is one of its progeny.

'Darley Leopard' ABCN 3896. *Not released*

Parents not disclosed
Long floral tube spotted like a leopard. Soft pale salmon orange pink petals, outer petals with greenish yellow midstripe. Sepals brownish with magenta midstripe. Stigma and style yellow. Filaments orange. Scented.

'Darley Lilac' ABCN 2210. *Not released*

CF4357: 'Darley Peach' × Johnson's unnamed hybrid
Hybridised in 1978, it has still not offset after 30 years. Long thin-tubed flowers. Petals magenta purple with darker edge and veined in deep magenta. Radiating sepals, bronze, tipped purple. Stigma greenish yellow. Style green. Filaments magenta. Very attractive hybrid.

'Darley Peach' *ABCN 3277. 1980*

CF4385: 'Darley Apricot' × ('Green Gold' × *Echinopsis kermesina*)
Flowers with yellowish orange narrow petals shading to peach at the centre. Stigma and style yellow. Filaments orange. Very attractive flowered hybrid with similarities to 'Lisa' and 'King Midas'.

'Darley Pearl' *ABCN 2330. 1983*

'Buttermilk' × 'Lemonade'
Large silvery pinkish flowers like the sheen on a pearl. Stigma and style cream. Filaments white. This is the same cross as 'Darley Queen' and is a selection out of hundreds of seedlings. Like 'Darley Queen' this hybrid has clear links with *Echinopsis oxygona*. The flowers are improved and the plant body is easily distinguishable, having shorter spines than *E. oxygona*.

'Darley Pinwheel' *ABCN 4072. 1995*

Parents not disclosed
Small long-tubed, wheel-shaped flowers with petals radiating like spokes. Petals pale salmon magenta, throat intense yellow. Stigma white. Style greenish. Filaments yellow. Scented. A useful parent which has produced a series of interesting hybrids such as 'Starlight'.

'Darley Queen' *ABCN 2204. 1983*

'Buttermilk' × 'Lemonade'
Huge flowers, 25cm long and 10cm in diameter. Petals deep fuchsia pink with a hint of white. Stigma and style white. Filaments cream. Scented.

A complicated hybrid descended from two American hybrids. The parents are two Abbey Brook named hybrids which themselves had been selected from hundreds of offspring. This hybrid has clear links to *Echinopsis oxygona* but is far superior.

'Darley Rose' *ABCN 2180. Hybridised in 1983 and named in 1988.*

CF7541: 'Ruffles' hybrid. The pollinator is not disclosed.
Inner petals pinkish lavender with orange midstripe, outer petals shading to pale orange. Filaments crimson, darkening at the centre of the flower making the centre look deep crimson. Inner petals slightly ruffled. Stigma and style yellow. Stunning.

'Darley Sunbeam' *ABCN 2676. 1985*

CF2368: 'Green Gold' × 'Terracotta' (cross made by Margaret Martin in 1977) Creamy white petals with a prominent golden yellow midstripe. Stigma pale yellow, style greenish. Filaments creamy white. Very distinctive. Highly scented.

In many ways similar to 'Cleopatra' but with different parents. Differs from 'Cleopatra' by the petal shape, paler flower colour and a less prominent midstripe.

'Darley Sunrise' *ABCN 2244. 1988*

'Ruffles' hybrid. Pollinator is not disclosed
Short-tubed, wide-opening flowers 10cm in diameter. Inner petals pale orange suffused with pink. Outer petals lavender pink. Sepals orange tinged bronze. Stigma white. Style green. Filaments orange and crimson. Scented.

The influence of 'Ruffles' is all apparent. Another stunning hybrid and my patience after 20 years of waiting is beginning to pay off. The real beauty about this flower is the folded and ruffled petals, sometimes completely obscuring the throat. This phenomenon only rarely occurs in *Echinopsis* species; I have seen ruffled petals only once, in *E. mamillosa*.

'Darley Sunset' *ABCN 2169. 1978*

CF4357: 'Darley Peach' × Johnson's unnamed hybrid
Flowers of deep magenta rose, outer petals violet. Stigma and style cream. Filaments orange. Same cross as 'Darley Lilac' but an entirely different sort of hybrid. Compare the photographs of the flowers. *(See page 28.)*

'Delicate' *ABCN 2313. 1986*

Echinopsis eyriesii × 'Paramount Pink'
Long-tubed flowers. Pure white petals with a delicate magenta pink midstripe. Very distinctive. Stigma, style and filaments white. Throat green. Adult plants almost spineless. Scented.

'Derbyshire Sunset' *ABCN 5904. 2007*

AB3697: 'Ruffles' × 'Ruffles II'. Hybridised in 1995
Large wide open flowers. Petals salmon orange with yellowish midline, each petal edged in reddish orange. Sepals pale orange with broad median line of greenish bronze. Stigma yellow. Style green. Filaments orange.

Very free-flowering hybrid with beautiful flowers. I now have two different plants of 'Ruffles' and this is the first selected hybrid produced when they are crossed.

'Electric' *ABCN 5085. 2002*

AB2874: (ABCN 3722 [which is a complex 4× hybrid] × Johnson's unnamed hybrid) × 'Crimson Glow'

Stunning long-tubed wide-opening flowers. Petals bright crimson red, inner petals with broad margins of vivid magenta pink. Outer petals with orange midstripe. Sepals with orange median stripe. Stigma crimson. Style pink. Filaments crimson magenta.

This is one of my most exciting hybrids. Unfortunately the flower is sterile, although the pollen is viable. Over several seasons it has stubbornly refused to set seed even when pollinated with a wide variety of pollen donors. It has also refused to offset, but I have not yet resorted to the beheading technique. Fortunately its pollen has set seed on a number of other hybrids. The results of this seed, provided it germinates, are awaited with interest during the next 10 years.

'Eleanor' ABCN 6041. 1996

CF2361: 'Peach Monarch' × 'Terracotta' (cross made by Margaret Martin in 1977)

Beautiful narrow, radiating, pointed, salmon pink petals. Centre of flower pale orange, outer petals with deep magenta midstripe. Stigma white. Style yellow. Filaments pale yellow. Named for Eleanor Marsh, a family friend.

Fearn's Petite Hybrids ABCN 5071. 2006

Echinopsis arachnacantha salmon flowered form (this is a hybrid, possibly *E. arachnacantha* yellow flowered × *E. ancistrophora*) × *Lobivia backebergii* subsp. *schieliana*

This cross produced 120 different seedlings, all small flowered (flowers only 1 to 1.5cm in diameter) but in a wide range of flower colours: pure white, orange, pink, red, lilac and magenta. A few seedlings were bicoloured with a white centre. Some seedlings have a purple stigma and many are sterile. Rather than name them individually, I much prefer to refer them as a single name. They are very floriferous and remain in flower for many months of the year. They are ideal as a beginner's or garden centre plant, as they are easy to grow and flower.

'Flamingo' *ABCN 5082. 2002*

'Princess Margaret' × Johnson's unnamed hybrid
Long-tubed flowers with many narrow, overlapping and crimped petals, pinkish salmon shading to pale salmon at the tips. Petals at the centre with prominent orange midstripe. Stigma and style magenta. Filaments pinkish orange. Scented.

'Gilly's Favourite' *ABCN 5599. 2005*

'Pink Camay' × 'Marie'
Large magenta flowers with deep crimson magenta midstripe. Stigma and style cream. Filaments pink. Scented. A large and beautiful flowered hybrid. Selected by and named for my wife Gill.

'Golden Eye' *ABCN 3245. 1990*

'Darley Gold' hybrid, a sibling of 'My Rosalie'
Short-tubed flowers varying in colour. Petals deep salmon orange red, shading to golden yellow at the centre. Sepals yellowish bronze. Stigma and style cream. Filaments yellow.

There appears to be two distinct layers of stamens which are fuzzy and twisted making the flowers sterile as a pollinator. The flowers do set seed when pollinated. Unusually on this cultivar there is often great variation in flower colour produced on the same plant at the same time. Sometimes all yellow or all pale orange flowers are produced. This phenomenon has been noticed on very few of my other hybrids.

'Gold Star' *ABCN 2688. 1988*

CF2364: 'Green Gold' × Peach Monarch' (cross made by Margaret Martin in 1977)
Long-tubed flowers. Inner petals deep golden yellow, outer petals and sepals shading to lavender peach. Stigma and style pale yellow. Filaments yellow. Scented.

In many ways similar to 'Darley Gold' but it has much stronger spination.

'Golden Fleece' *ABCN 5610. 2005*

AB3078: *Echinopsis arachnacantha* × *E. calorubra* F_2
This is another interesting hybrid which introduces the colour yellow into the *E. calorubra* complex. Smallish flowers of deep golden yellow with a hint of red. Sepals radiating, reddish bronze. Stigma and style yellow. Filaments yellow.

'Golden Progress' *ABCN 4455. 2001*

CF178: 'Green Gold' × *Echinopsis kermesina*

Large flowers, inner petals deep golden yellow with median line of reddish pink. Outer petals yellow suffused with orange. Sepals edged with bronze. Stigma golden yellow. Style greenish yellow. Filaments golden yellow. Highly scented.
This is a selection from one of the very first crosses made in 1973. The genes from hybrids like this one, for example, scent, colours yellow and magenta, are firmly embedded in many later hybrids.

'Goldie' *ABCN 2176. 1976*

Echinopsis aurea × 'Green Gold'
Attractive spiny plants, columnar with age. Golden yellow flowers. Stigma and style yellow. Filaments yellow shading to red at the centre of the flower. One of the first Abbey Brook hybrids.

'Green Ice' *ABCN 2310. 1984*

CF2105: 'Buttermilk' × 'Paramount Yellow'. Hybridised in 1978. Flowers pure white with frilled edged petals. Outer petals with a green midstripe. Throat green. Stigma, style and filaments white. Highly scented. Spiny plants with yellowish green bodies.

'Janet' *ABCN 5600. 2005*

'Pink Camay' × 'Shirley'

Large flowers deep magenta with a faint orange midstripe. Sepals tipped green. Stigma, style and filaments white. Highly scented. Adult plants almost spineless.

Named for Janet Walters, a long time friend from the Nottingham branch of the BCSS.

'Jo' *ABCN 5911. 2006*

'Ruffles' × collection

Superb large, long-tubed flowers. Petals in tones of crimson, magenta and orange. Each petal is crimped and folded, with a prominent midstripe. Sepals pale crimson with a prominent greenish midstripe. Stigma cream. Style green. Filaments white. Scented.

This hybrid first flowered at Hampton Court Flower Show in 2006 and was seen in flower on *BBC Gardeners' World*. It is named for Joanna Jones, the Fund Raising Officer of Plant Heritage. It is one of the best of my latest hybrids.

'Jennifer Ann' *ABCN 4250. 1999*

CF7545: *Echinopsis arachnacantha* × *E. calorubra* F_2
Inner petals cream with pale lemon yellow midstripe. Sepals pale green with brown margins. Stigma and style white. Filaments cream. One of the second generation of hybrids of the revolutionary cross between two distinct groups of *Echinopsis* species. Jennifer Ann is a nice name for an attractive flower.

'Juliette' *ABCN 3687. 1999*

CF8261: ('Lemonade' × 'Darley Queen') × ('Green Gold' × 'Terracotta')
Complex multi-parented hybrid. Very large flowers of deep salmon orange with yellowish orange midstripe. Stigma and style pale yellow. Filaments lavender pink. Scented.

'King Midas' *ABCN 4183. 1998*

CF8261: ('Lemonade' × 'Darley Queen') × ('Green Gold' × 'Terracotta')
Complex multi-parented hybrid. Large long-tubed flowers. Petals deep orange and yellow. Sepals yellowish bronze. Stigma yellow. Style greenish. Filaments orange. Scented.

Fabulous flowers which make a real splash of colour in the glasshouse. The colour is similar to the classic epiphyllum hybrid of the same name raised in 1939 by Cactus Pete in California.

'Lemon Custard' *ABCN 3279. Not released*

'Goldie' × collection

Large flowers, intense buttercup yellow with broad obtuse pointed petals and darker yellow midstripe. Outer sepals tinged bronze. Stigma yellow, style greenish. Filaments yellow. Scented. Very attractive almost spineless plants. Spines very short and black and only 3-5 spines to each areole.

This is a very interesting hybrid, as its spination seems to be unique. It is totally different from 'Goldie', one of its parents.

'Lemonade' *ABCN 4381. 1979*

'Green Gold' × 'Golden Dream'

Large flowers 20cm long and 10cm diameter. Long narrow pointed petals, lemon yellow with a darker yellow midstripe. Stigma and style yellow. Filaments yellow. Highly scented. A very early hybrid, but still worth growing for its scent.

'Lisa' *ABCN 3288. 1996*

'Golden Dream' × collection

A superb long-tubed orange salmon flowered hybrid. Stigma and style yellowish. Filaments salmon pink. Scented. Distinct colour.

As good as 'King Midas'. Named for Lisa Brownlee, a long serving member of staff who looks after 'the shop' when I am away.

'Lotus Blossom' *ABCN 2301. Not released*

Echinopsis subdenudata × *E. kermesina* F_1

Rounded petals of lavender pink with deep lavender midstripe. Very large attractive flowers. Stigma and style creamy yellow. Filaments white.

Another very early hybrid cross between two distinct species. Unfortunately it does not offset, but has been used to produce many other beautiful hybrids, as it is fully fertile.

'Lyndsey' *ABCN 2607. 2000*

CF6013: 'Darley Rose' × collection Bi-coloured flowers, ruffled petals of delicate lavender pink with a broad orange midstripe. Stigma and style yellow. Filaments lavender. Scented.

This hybrid dates from 1983. Named for Lyndsey, one of the daughters of Sarah Bater, a long serving nursery worker. This hybrid sometimes, but not always, has a 'Ruffles' type of flower. The pollen donor is most likely to be 'Ruffles'.

'Margot Fonteyn' *ABCN 3339. 1993*

CF4357: 'Darley Peach' × Johnson's unnamed hybrid

Short-tubed, broad flesh pink inner petals, outer petals pinkish bronze with orange midstripe. Stigma pink. Style crimson. Filaments white. Scented. A beautiful hybrid named for a famous ballerina. Hybridised in 1978 and named 15 years later.

'Marie' *ABCN 4365. 1998*

CF8261: ('Lemonade' × 'Darley Queen') × ('Green Gold' × 'Terracotta')

Same cross as 'King Midas' and 'Juliette'. Deep salmon pink suffused with lavender. Inner petals with orange midstripe. Stigma and style yellowish. Filaments crimson.

Named for Marie Greatorex, a long serving nursery worker, now in happy retirement.

'Matlock Gem' *ABCN 2575. 1986*

'Ruffles' × collection

Medium tubed flowers, petals flesh pink with orange yellow midstripe. Outer petals tinged magenta. Stigma white. Style yellow. Filaments yellow. Scented.

'Matlock Sunset' *ABCN 2211. 1984*

Parents not disclosed

Long-tubed flowers, deep reddish rose, outer petals tinged orange. Petals veined in reddish violet. Edges of inner petals tinged magenta. Stigma yellow. Style greenish yellow. Filaments orange. Scented.

Fabulous coloured flowers. I have hybridised this cultivar with 'Darley Sunrise'. I am awaiting the first flowers with great interest.

'My Rosalie' *ABCN 4366. Not released*

'Darley Gold' hybrid, a sibling of 'Golden Eye'.
Short-tubed flowers of orange red with a prominent white throat. Broad obtuse petals with crimped edges. Outer petals and sepals pinkish mauve, with a yellowish midline. Small flowered. Stigma yellow. Style green. Filaments white. Scented. Male sterile. Filaments are in a ring, making the throat look white. This hybrid is not named for any particular person.

'Mystic Moon' *ABCN 4181. 2000*

CF2361: 'Peach Monarch' × 'Terracotta' (cross made by Margaret Martin in 1977)
Pale lemon yellow inner petals with darker yellow midstripe. Outer petals pinkish brown. Stigma and style cream. Filaments yellow. Scented.

'Orange Blossom' *ABCN 3248. 1990*

'Ruffles' × collection

Flowers with broad petals with obtuse tips, pale flesh pinkish orange. Stigma and style cream. Filaments orange. Scented.

'Orange Garden' *ABCN 2272. 1986*

'Ruffles' × collection

Large long-tubed flowers. Petals deep salmon orange. Stigma and style yellow. Filaments deep orange magenta. Scented.

'Orange Ice Cream' *ABCN 2242. 1989*

CF2367: *E. eyriesii* × 'Red Meteor' (cross made by Margaret Martin in 1977)
Pale orange with yellow midstripe, edges of petals dark orange. Stigma and style yellow. Filaments orange shading to lilac. Scented. A beautiful multi-flowered almost spineless hybrid.

'Orange Queen' *ABCN 2587. 1988*

'Golden Dream × 'Lemonade'
Long-tubed flowers. Deep yellow inner petals with magenta midstripe, outer petals reddish orange tinged with magenta. Stigma and style pale yellow. Filaments deep yellow. Scented.
Flowered for the first time at Chelsea Flower Show in 1988.

'Orange Sensation' *ABCN 2292. 1978*

CF3320: *Echinopsis arachnacantha* × *E. calorubra* F_1

Deep orange with a dark magenta midstripe. Petals edged with magenta. Sepals greenish bronze. Stigma and style greenish. Filaments orange.

One of a superb range of hybrids from the first ever successful cross between large flowered and small flowered species. Not named until 1987. *Echinopsis arachnacantha* is a small yellow flowered species, and *Echinopsis calorubra* is large growing with large multicoloured flowers. The hybrid is small flowered 10cm long and 5cm in diameter. The plants do not grow tall and offset freely from the base. The individual heads are 3 or 4 times the size of *E. arachnacantha* but are small in comparison with *E. calorubra*.

'Party Frock' *ABCN 5611. 2005*

'Ruffles' × collection

Very attractive large flowered hybrid. Flowers deep reddish salmon with orange midstripe. The outer petals in particular are crimped. Sepals orange with green midline. Stigma and style yellow. Filaments crimson.

'Peach Sundae' *ABCN 4377. Not released*

CF4009: *Echinopsis orozasana* × *E. calorubra* F$_1$
Deep orange red flowers with lighter orange midstripe, petals sharply pointed sepals magenta bronze. Stigma and style white. Filaments red. Scented. An early hybrid made in 1979 which has never offset.

'Pineapple Poll' *ABCN 2212. 2005*

'King Midas' × collection
Petals orange yellow with a darker midline. Stigma and style yellow. Filaments deep orange. Scented. A brilliant outstanding hybrid which makes a lovely splash of colour in the glasshouse.

'Pink Camay' *ABCN 2240. 1986*

CF2368: 'Green Gold' × 'Terracotta' (cross made by Margaret Martin in 1977) Sharply pointed petals, delicate pink with darker midstripe. Stigma and style cream. Filaments pink.

'Pink Champagne' *ABCN 2228. 1986*

'Titania' × collection

Large long-tubed flowers. Flesh pink petals with yellowish orange midstripe. Stigma white, style greenish. Filaments white. Scented. Plants almost spineless with tiny white areoles and very attractive flowers.

'Pink Glory' *ABCN 2325. 1987*

Parents not disclosed
Short-tubed flowers. Petals deep magenta pink with prominent orange midstripe. Highly scented. Stigma white, style green. Filaments yellow. Unusually the filaments coalesce to form the beginning of a hymen. A hybrid with outstandingly colourful flowers.

'Pink Nymph' *ABCN 3541. 1993*

CF2361: 'Peach Monarch' × Terracotta' (cross made by Margaret Martin in 1977)
Long narrow tubed flowers with deep rose pink petals with orange midstripe. Outer petals and sepals with a greenish bronze midstripe. Stigma and style white. Filaments pink. Scented.

'Primrose Beauty' *ABCN 5905. 2007*

AB2858: *Echinopsis calorubra* × *E. arachnacantha* F$_4$
Very large flowers in cup and saucer form. Primrose yellow with spreading outer petals and sepals. Sepals yellow tipped bronze. Stigma and style green, filaments pale green. Scented.

This, after 40 years' work, is one of the latest batch of my *Echinopsis* hybrids. I have at last produced an attractive *E. calorubra* type plant with very large yellow flowers for the first time.

'Princess Diana' *ABCN 2315. 1983*

Johnson's un-named hybrid × collection
Pink petals with orange midstripe. Stigma and style pale yellow. Filaments lavender. Scented. I can only speculate what the other parent is. A very early hybrid with very pretty flowers. Named in 1983 for the Princess of Wales. Like 'Pink Glory' this hybrid has the beginnings of a hymen by fusion of the filaments.

'Princess Margaret' *ABCN 2173. 1983*

CF4363: CF2366 × CF2102

This is a very complicated hybrid. CF2366: ('Green Gold' × collection, a cross made by Margaret Martin in 1977, salmon flowers) × CF2102: (ABCN 124 × *E. kermesina* hybridised in 1977, white flowers). ABCN 124 is an *Echinopsis* hybrid of unknown origin, white flowers).

'Princess Margaret' has long-tubed flowers. Lavender pink with prominent deep lavender midstripe. Outer petals with orange midstripe. Stigma white, style green. Filaments white. Scented.

Named for H.M. The Queen's late sister.

'Raspberry Sorbet' *ABCN 4378. 2000*

AB2851: 'Paramount Yellow' × collection
Long-tubed flowers with vivid magenta petals with orange midstripe. Outer petals magenta bronze. Stigma yellow. Style green. Filaments orange magenta. Scented.

'Really Pretty' *ABCN 3733. 1992*

'Ruffles' × 'Delicate'
Frilled pink inner petals, purple midstripe, outer petals salmon orange. Long-tubed flowers. Stigma white, style green. Filaments cream.

'Ruffles' ABCN 2311. 1987. Not released

Parentage not disclosed

Sensational unique flowers. Delicate pale orange, ruffled, double petals covering the centre of the flower like a carnation. Sepals orange, tinged bronze. Stigma and style yellow. Filaments pinkish. Scented.

When this hybrid first flowered in 1987 it was the only one out of a batch of seedlings with this characteristic flower form. As far as we are aware nobody else has produced a similar hybrid.

It was not until 15 years later that another identical plant appeared which I named 'Ruffles II'. 'Derbyshire Sunset' is the first distinct hybrid produced by crossing 'Ruffles' and 'Ruffles II'.

Fortunately both the 'Ruffles' plants are fertile and we are now making extensive use of their pollen in seed production. 'Ruffles' has already produced a whole series of beautiful hybrids, and there are more in the pipeline.

'Ruffles' plants are not for sale and the parentage remains a secret. It is likely that there are other plants like 'Ruffles' in the world, as over the years we have distributed many thousands of seeds and unflowered seedlings. The growers may not realise what an unusual plant they possess.

'Rufflette' *ABCN 3934. 1993. Not released*

AB2674: 'Matlock Sunset' × 'Ruffles'
Flowers ruffled like 'Ruffles' but multicoloured. Petals salmon pink, magenta and orange. Sepals pale orange tinged bronze. Stigma and style purple. Filaments deep pinkish orange.

Like one of its parents, this is another sensational flower and in many ways even more attractive because it is multicoloured. We currently have a crop of seedlings of this hybrid crossed with 'Ruffles'. Some of these have started to flower in 2008 with a range of flower colours and combinations, but not properly 'ruffled'. One of these seedlings has pure white flowers. All of them have been recrossed and another generation will be grown. The flowers of the remainder of the crop are awaited with great interest. A ruffled yellow flowered one would be spectacular. 'Rufflette' plants are not for sale.

'Sangria' *ABCN 5083. 2002*

'Ruffles' × collection

Large multicoloured flowers. Petals salmon magenta and yellow. Petals darker at the centre, much paler to nearly white at the tips. Stigma and style greenish. Filaments orange. Scented.

'Sarah' *ABCN 4367. 2000*

CF3090: *Echinopsis orozasana* × collection

Large flowers of buttercup yellow, outer petals cream suffused with lavender. Stigma white, style greenish. Filaments deep yellow. Scented.

A selection from an early hybrid and named for Sarah Bater, a long serving nursery worker. *E. orozasana* is a white flowered species related to *E. calorubra*. Unfortunately I did not note the pollen donor (it was 30 years ago) and I have no idea what it was. A yellow flowered offspring from this cross is most unexpected as *E. orozasana* is the seed parent.

'Sheryl' *ABCN 5081. 2002*

'Golden Dream' × 'Ruffles'
Large long-tubed many-petalled flowers, creamy white with a hint of pink. Petals long and narrow with sharply pointed tips. Sepals yellowish bronze. Stigma and style white. Filaments greenish.

Named for Sheryl, daughter of Lisa Brownlee, a long serving nursery worker. The flower looks nothing like either parent. These are both complex hybrids and 'Golden Dream' possibly has *E. oxygona* in its parentage.

'Shirley' *ABCN 3247. 1990*

CF2361: 'Peach Monarch' × 'Terracotta' (cross made by Margaret Martin in 1977)
Large flowers with magenta pink petals with an orange midstripe. Stigma and style cream. Filaments white. Scented.

Named for Shirley Davison, a long serving Councillor with me on Darley Dale Town Council at a time when we were both involved in twinning Darley Dale with the French town of Onzain in the Loire Valley.

'Shot Silk' *ABCN 2203. 1986*

'Green Gold' × collection
Very large long-tubed, gorgeous flowers of deep vermilion, orange and crimson. Stigma cream. Style green. Filaments orange. This is one of my best hybrids.

'Son of Orange Sensation' *ABCN 4380*

'Orange Sensation' × CF3320. Hybridised in 1987.
Very short-tubed flowers, intense deep orange, cup and saucer type flowers. Each petal edged in deep orange magenta. Outer sepals radiating, orange bronze. Stigma and style yellow. Filaments orange.

This hybrid was produced by backcrossing 'Orange Sensation' with a yellow flowered seedling from the same generation. Individual heads are like its parents but 3 or 4 times the size of the original *E. arachnacantha*.

'Starlight' ABCN 2285. 1989

'Darley Pinwheel' × collection

Strikingly beautiful flowers. Very many narrow petals, pale lavender pink with a deeper lavender orange midstripe. Filaments white. Stigma and style cream. Filaments white. Scented. Plants growing tall with age. Spineless with large white felted areoles.

'Starlight Express' ABCN 5612. 2005

'Starlight' × 'Darley Pinwheel'

Long narrow channelled petals radiating like the spokes of a wheel. Inner petals pale salmon suffused with magenta. Outer petals and sepals pale salmon bronze. Stigma white, style green. Filaments yellow, making the centre of the flower appear yellow. Scented.

'Sterling Silver' *ABCN 4376. 1999*

CF4413: 'Goldie' × collection

Small silvery white flowers with a hint of lavender. Outer petals with green stripe. Petals change colour to deep lavender orange as the flower ages. Stigma and style white. Filaments white. Sterile.

'Sunny Jim' *ABCN 4279. 1988*

CF4378: 'Goldie' × 'Darley Queen'

Very large flowers. Stunning colour. Golden yellow inner petals shading to apricot at tips, with a magenta midstripe. Stigma, style and filaments yellow.

Hybridised in 1978, a cross between two unlikely parents has produced a stunning hybrid. *Echinopsis aurea*, one of the parents of 'Goldie', is a relatively small flowered species. The parents of 'Darley Queen' are all large flowered species. Hybrids between the two groups do not occur very easily.

'Streaky' *ABCN 5601. 2001*

'Ruffles' × collection

Very variable flowers that seem to change with each season. Wide open flowers with a very narrow throat, varying from pale pink *(below)* to deep orange *(left)*, with streaky lines of yellow. Black hairy corolla tube. Stigma yellow, style greenish yellow. Filaments pale orange or white. Scented. Male sterile.

'Summer Carnival' *ABCN 5912. 2007*

'Shot Silk' × collection
Plants almost spineless with white felted areoles. Large flowers, orange and magenta petals with a crimson midstripe. Stigma and style yellowish. Filaments reddish orange. Scented. A very attractive new hybrid.

'Summer Glory' *ABCN 4182. 1998*

CF2361: 'Peach Monarch' × 'Terracotta' (cross made by Margaret Martin in 1977).
Pale peach with apricot stripe, outer petals pinkish brown. Stigma white, style yellow. Filaments yellow.

This is the same cross as 'Mystic Moon' but a totally different coloured flower.

'Susan' *ABCN 3697. 1993*

CF7574: *Echinopsis calorubra* × *E. arachnacantha* F$_3$
A hybrid cross made 15 years after the first effort. It pays to continue and keep records! Cup and saucer type flowers, deep orange, outer petals and sepals brownish orange with orange midstripe. Stigma and style green. Filaments deep orange.

'Swan Lake' *ABCN 5906. 2007*

Echinopsis leucorhodantha × *E. calorubra* F$_3$
Large flowers, petals bi-coloured, inner face deep lavender pink, reverse side silvery pink. Flowers appear double as there are many petals. Outer petals and sepals radiating, pink with yellowish midline. Stigma and style greenish. Filaments white.

A third generation hybrid of one of my very first efforts. Its flower colour is totally unlike any of its parents.

'Tango' *ABCN 4793. 2005*

AB2851: 'Paramount Yellow' × collection

Large flowers, salmon orange with lighter orange yellow midstripe. Stigma yellow, style green. Filaments orange shading to green. Scented. Beautiful flowers.

A selected seedling from a cross made in 1993. Same cross as 'Raspberry Sorbet'.

'Titania' *ABCN 2307. Not released*

Parents not disclosed

Very large flowers, pale salmon pink with prominent orange midstripe. Sepals blackish bronze. Stigma and style cream. Filaments white. Scented. Columnar black-spined plants. Most unusual.

'Turkish Delight' *ABCN 4784. 2001*

AB2841: 'Margot Fonteyn' × 'Pink Nymph'

A very beautiful hybrid. Large flowers with short tube. Broad petals, pale pink with distinct orange magenta midstripe. Stigma and style cream. Filaments white. Scented.

Another with complicated parentage, involving at least six hybrids which may account for the plants being distinctly variegated.

'Van Gogh' *ABCN 5907. 2007*

Parents not disclosed
Inner petals salmon orange, outer petals pale orange with a hint of magenta. Stigma yellow. Style greenish. Filaments orange. Attractive short-spined plants with white felted areoles.

'Wedding Silk' *ABCN 4000. 1989*

CF6017: 'Buttercup' × collection
Very pale silky straw yellow petals. Stigma and style white. Filaments white.
Compare this hybrid with 'Sterling Silver'. They are both white flowered hybrids produced from different seed parents, both of which are yellow flowered. Hybridised in 1981.

The × *Trichoechinopsis* and × *Tricholobiviopsis* hybrids

These are hybrids between *Trichocereus* and *Echinopsis* and between *Trichocereus*, *Lobivia* and *Echinopsis* respectively.

Propagating these hybrids is often only achieved by cutting whole stems into segments and rooting them. The offsets produced by these segments are then removed and rooted when large enough to handle. As a result, because of the time involved, many of these hybrids are not yet in commerce.

× *Trichoechinopsis* 'Abbey Brook' *ABCN 2610. 1990*

CF6009: *Trichocereus thelegonus* × *Echinopsis kermesina* F_1
Very large flowers, 22cm long and 12cm in diameter. Lavender pink petals with broad white margins. Throat green. Sepals reflexed, narrow, lavender bronze. Stigma and style yellowish. Filaments white. Scented.
Together with × *T*. 'Garden News', this hybrid is one of the first × *Trichoechinopsis* hybrids produced at Abbey Brook. The plants grow tall with age and branch freely from the base. The original plant is now over a metre tall and produces 12 to 15 flowers at the same time. The plant needs firmly staking otherwise it takes on the habit of its *Trichocereus* parent and creeps along the ground.

'Chatsworth' *ABCN 2302. 1983*

CF7579: *Trichocereus lamprochlorus* × *Echinopsis* 'Brian's Choice'
Large impressive flowers. Broad, deep salmon pink petals with a hint of magenta. Outer petals narrow and spreading, deep pink. Sepals narrow, greenish bronze. Stigma white and style green. Filaments pink. Scented.
A stunning hybrid when in flower that never fails to impress visitors when they see it. Named for Chatsworth, one of the great houses of England, where the genius of Sir Joseph Paxton was encouraged.

'Chelsea Girl' *ABCN 2691. 1988*

'Garden News' × collection

Large flowers 20cm long and 12cm in diameter. Petals golden yellow, and as the flower ages each petal is edged with orange. Sepals narrow and reflexed, yellow with median band of bronze. Stigma and style yellow. Filaments yellow. Scented.

This hybrid flowered for the first time at Chelsea Flower Show in 1988. According to Professor Gröner it is the first reported hybrid with yellow flowers in this group. It would appear that these yellow flowered hybrids only appear in the second and subsequent generations, and that nobody previously had had the luck to have chosen the right parents. It is even luckier as I do not know the identity of the pollen donor.

After this first success, other yellow flowered × *Trichoechinopsis* hybrids have appeared. 'Chelsea Sunshine', 'Golden Wedding', and 'Cariba' are all second generation yellow flowered hybrids. It is interesting to note that *Trichocereus thelegonus* × *Echinopsis kermesina* (i.e. × *T.* 'Abbey Brook') in the second and subsequent generations has never produced a yellow flowered hybrid. 'Ruth Fearn', a purple and white flowered hybrid, is an example of one of these second generation hybrids.

'Cariba' *ABCN 4280. 2000*

'Garden News' × *Trichocereus lamprochlorus*
Deep golden yellow petals, outer petals with brownish magenta midstripe at tips. Stigma yellow. Style pink. Filaments golden yellow. A second generation hybrid with yellow flowers.

'Chelsea Sunshine' *ABCN 4382. 1995*

'Chelsea Girl' × 'Garden News' Intense yellow flowers, sepals tinged with orange. Stigma and filaments yellow. Attractive spiny large growing clump forming plants. Plants were available commercially for the first time in 2008.

'Fulviruff' *ABCN 4383. 1993*

(*Trichocereus fulvilanus* × *Echinopsis ?eyriesii*) × 'Ruffles'
Gigantic short-tubed flowers. Petals pale salmon orange, slightly ruffled. Stigma and style yellow. Filaments yellow. Scented. Distinctive tall growing plants with long black spines.

The original × *Trichoechinopsis* hybrid that I have was given to me by Gordon Foster of Oakdene Nurseries, Barnsley. It is a tall growing almost spineless hybrid, freely offsetting from the base, and with large pure white flowers. I had tried on a number of occasions to hybridise *T. fulvilanus* with *Echinopsis* species and hybrids and failed totally. Fortunately Gordon was successful and I thank him for his generosity in giving me a plant. He cannot remember which *Echinopsis* he used, but second generation seedlings often have no spines and white felted areoles just like *E. eyriesii*. This supports my contention that this was the most likely parent.

'Fulviruff' is the first selection of my cross of Gordon's hybrid with 'Ruffles'. From hybridising 'Fulviruff' and 'Ruffles' another orange flowered hybrid has appeared which is almost spineless like the original hybrid. This hybrid I have called 'Darley Oakdene'.

Late in 2007 I at last managed to hybridise *T. fulvilanus* with an *Echinopsis*. I used *E. kermesina*, as in my first × *Trichoechinopsis* cross that flowered in 1990; × *Trichoechinopsis* 'Abbey Brook'.

'Darley Oakdene' ABCN 6043. 2007

'Fulviruff' × 'Ruffles'
Large short-tubed flowers, deep salmon orange with a hint of magenta. Sepals reflexed, greenish bronze. Stigma and style yellow. Filaments orange. Distinctive tall growing almost spineless plants with prominent white felted areoles. Named for Gordon Foster of Oakdene Nurseries.

'Garden News' ABCN 3727. 1980

Echinopsis kermesina × *Trichocereus schickendantzii* F_1
Very large orange red flowers. Large growing spiny plants, clump forming from the base. Easy to grow and flower. One of the first of my × *Trichoechinopsis* hybrids.
A colour photograph of this hybrid was printed on the front cover of the newspaper 'Garden News' in August 1980 and this hybrid was subsequently named for the newspaper.

'Gillian' *ABCN 4790. 2001*

AB4217: 'Garden News' × *Lobivia purpureominiata*
Very large short-tubed flowers. Petals pinkish magenta, petals edged in darker magenta. Outer petals and sepals scarlet red. Stigma and style white. Filaments crimson. Like 'Papa Dip' and 'Millennium', it is another selection from this interesting cross.

'Golden Wedding' *ABCN 4773. 2001*

AB2948: *Trichocereus lamprochlorus* × *Lobivia huascha* var. *grandiflora* F_2 Short-tubed deep golden yellow flowers. Stigma and style yellow. Filaments yellow. Scented. It is interesting that yellow flowered hybrids occur in the second generation hybrids, but not in the first. Even then you have to choose the right parents.

'Harlequin' *ABCN 6044. 1991*

AB2948: *Trichocereus lamprochlorus* × *Lobivia huascha* var. *grandiflora* F$_2$
Very large cup and saucer shaped flowers. Inner petals deep orange, outer petals and sepals spreading, lighter orange with yellowish midstripe. Filaments orange. Stigma and style yellow. Spectacular when in flower. Another selected seedling from the same cross as 'Golden Wedding'.

'Les Parkin' *ABCN 5903. 2007*

Trichocereus lamprochlorus × 'Garden News' F$_2$
Large many-petalled flowers crimson red on the inner surface, and silvery red on the backs of the petals. The petals are channelled and curve inwards. The floral tube has prominent green scales and black hairs. Stigma and style yellowish. Filaments crimson.
An unusual and very attractive flower, named for Les who has volunteered his help in maintaining my Plant Heritage National Plant Collections for many years.

'Loganberry Pete' *ABCN 6098. 2008*

'Garden News' × *Lobivia purpureominiata* F$_2$
Highly coloured small-flowered hybrid with short tube covered in black hairs. Petals rounded, deep orange. Sepals orange bronze. Stigma and style yellow. Filaments deep crimson. Small growing plant, freely offsetting at the base. Named for an Abbey Brook customer of more than 30 years and an enthusiastic collector of my *Echinopsis* hybrids.

'Millennium' *ABCN 4375. 2000*

AB4127: 'Garden News' × *Lobivia purpureominiata*
Very dark crimson petals with a hint of magenta. Flowered for the first time at Easter 2000. The intensity of colour in the petals of this hybrid is distinctive, and unlike that of any of my other × *Trichoechinopsis* and × *Tricholobiviopsis* hybrids.

'Papa Dip' *ABCN 5902. 2006*

AB4127: 'Garden News' × *Lobivia purpureominiata*

Large broad-petalled crimson flowers. Outer petals and sepals narrow, crimson bronze. Stigma pale yellow. Style pink. Filaments blackish crimson making the throat appear black. Scented. Papa Dip, named for King Oliver, is one of my wife Gill's favourite Traditional Jazz tunes.

'Raspberry Ripple' *ABCN 4384. 1995*

'Garden News' × × *Trichoechinopsis* 'Abbey Brook'

Gigantic short-tubed flowers, petals white shading to deep pinkish magenta at the base. Filaments and stigma yellow. This hybrid is aptly named and is just like its ice cream counterpart.

'Ruth Fearn' *ABCN 5909. 2006*

Trichocereus thelegonus ×*Echinopsis kermesina* F$_2$

Large spectacular flowers. Deep lavender petals with a prominent white margin. Sepals narrow and radiating, deep magenta. Stigma and style creamy yellow. Filaments white.

This second, F$_2$ generation, produces plants which are much stouter and shorter than in the F$_1$ generation (× *Trichoechinopsis* 'Abbey Brook').

With its smaller growing habit when compared with its parents, this plant will become very popular, as its flowers are just as spectacular. A fitting tribute to 'mum' without her help and encouragement over many years, none of my work would have been possible. She died just short of her 95th birthday, having been a plantsperson all her life.

'Sir Joseph Paxton' *ABCN 5908. 2007*

AB2116: 'Garden News' × *Lobivia grandiflora*
Fat 13cm diameter stems growing tall and clumping with age. Gigantic flowers produced in profusion around the apex. Flowers 15cm long and 18cm in diameter. Fuchsia pink with broad petals with obtuse tips. Stigma yellow. Style pink. Filaments crimson.

Named for Sir Joseph Paxton, Victorian entrepreneur and Head Gardener at Chatsworth House. He designed and built for his family Darley House which is only 400 metres away from Abbey Brook where this hybrid was produced.
A suitable photograph is not available.

Analysis of Parentage

My records show that 44 species and hybrids have been used to produce the existing Abbey Brook hybrids. In addition the genes of another 30 or so are also in the mix, although they do not appear as a particular parent. They probably make up some of the unknown parents (included in the Check List as "× collection", a term used by epiphyllum hybridists when the flowers are pollinated with whatever was in flower in their collection at the time, but not specifically noted).

When checking through the parents of my named hybrids, less than half of the species and hybrids used in seed production have produced hybrids sufficiently different to be worthy of a name. I now have a much better idea of which species and hybrids to use.

Having now named 130 hybrids, the number of potential donors and receptors has risen dramatically. This fact increases the odds of producing good new hybrids because most of the parents now being used have already undergone a rigorous selection process.

When this is borne in mind, people who raise only a few seedlings have little chance of consistently producing *Echinopsis* hybrids of merit. This analysis is borne out when considering the thousands of named hybrids produced by epiphyllum growers. In the production of epiphyllum hybrids, a rigorous weeding out of inferior material has not always been made. As a result, only a small percentage of them are worth keeping. Take a tip from the rose breeders who grow fields full of seedlings in the hope of producing something new.

I have analysed my existing hybridisation data and produced out of curiosity, a top twelve list. A number of old American hybrids appear with 'Green Gold' at the top of the list.

Top twelve list of plants used as pollen donors or receptors from 1965 – 2007 in producing the Abbey Brook hybrids.

1	'Green Gold'	6	'Darley Queen'
2	'Terracotta'	7	*E. calorubra*
3	'Ruffles'	= 8	Johnson's unnamed hybrid
= 4	'Lemonade'	= 8	'Golden Dream'
= 4	*E. kermesina*	= 9	*E. arachnacantha*
5	'Garden News'	= 9	'Peach Monarch'

I predict that this list will change dramatically in the next ten years. 'Ruffles' will consolidate its position, to be joined by 'Darley Rose', 'Derbyshire Sunset', 'Derbyshire Sunrise', 'Turkish Delight' and 'Ruth Fearn'.

Plants used in the Production of Abbey Brook Echinopsis Hybrids

Details follow of some of the species and other hybrids that have been used in the last 40 years in the production of the Abbey Brook *Echinopsis* hybrids. It will be noticed that many of the following plant names have been changed in *The New Cactus Lexicon* (Hunt 2006). In the absence of DNA studies to back up these new combinations, I reserve judgement on these changes.

Of all of these species and hybrids, a Johnson's unnamed hybrid is probably the most important.

Echinopsis Johnson's unnamed hybrid

Parents unknown
Small crimson magenta flowers, sepals magenta bronze. Stigma deep crimson purple. Style crimson. Filaments crimson.

This had its origins in Johnson's Cactus Garden in California. It came to Abbey Brook with a number of other plants from a collection in Leicester in the early 1960s. It is a very interesting plant that was used extensively in my early hybrids. There is no data on its origin and we can only speculate as to what its parents are. Its genes are now firmly embedded in the Abbey Brook hybrids and 40 years later hybrids still appear with a purple stigma which reverts back to this original Johnson plant.

Species and other hybrids used as seed parents or pollen donors

Echinopsis ancistrophora
(E. leucorhodantha is probably another name for this species)

Small growing solitary plants with soft wavy spines. Flowers usually white, but often with pinkish outer petals and sepals. The relatively small flowers are produced in profusion. I originally hybridised these plants with the much larger growing and more colourful species *E. calorubra*. I persevered with these hybrids and in the second and third generation have produced two beautiful new hybrids, namely 'Ballet Dancers' and 'Swan Lake'.

Echinopsis arachnacantha

This is a very small growing, caespitose plant with small deep yellow flowers. My original plants came direct from Professor Martin Cardenas in Bolivia in the early 1960s. There is another very similar plant with dark red flowers which was called *E. torrecillasensis*, but this is now regarded as part of the variation of *E. arachnacantha*. Long before I started work on the larger *Echinopsis* species I hybridised these together. There is now a range of colour forms including orange, purple and white and also a larger growing salmon flowered form: a hybrid with *E. ancistrophora*. None of these plants have been given names. All these colour forms are easy to grow and flower and take up little space. I made the first successful attempt to hybridise these with one of the larger growing species. Fortunately I chose *E. calorubra*, which has yielded some very good hybrids, such as 'Golden Fleece' and 'Primrose Beauty' which introduce the colour yellow into the *E. calorubra* complex for the first time. I have also backcrossed these hybrids with *E. calorubra* and 'Jennifer Ann' is one of the results.

Latterly I have turned my attention back to this group and hybridised the salmon flowered hybrid of *E. arachnacantha* with *Lobivia backebergii* subsp. *schieliana*, which just happened to be in flower at the same time. This one cross produced 120 seedlings in a new range of small flowered multicoloured hybrids, which are in flower for 6 months of the year. I have called this new group Fearn's Petite Hybrids without naming them individually. Many of them are self sterile, often with a purple stigma.

Echinopsis aurea

In the past this species has often been classified as a *Lobivia*. It has relatively small yellow flowers. The plants are variable in spination, sometimes with long black spines (var. *fallax*); others have many silvery spines which have either been called var. *quinesensis* or var. *leucomalla*.

There is another plant with few spines and beautiful red flowers. This is probably distinct enough to retain its varietal status as var. *dobeana*. I have produced some new hybrids, as yet unflowered, using this as one of the parents. Two of my earliest hybrids 'Buttercup' and 'Goldie' have *E. aurea* in their parentage. In addition the Gates hybrid 'Golden Dream' probably has *E. aurea* in its parentage too.

Echinopsis callochrysea FR 985. ABCN 4023

A spiny tall growing species with golden yellow flowers. It has broad petals with elongated points at the tip. Stigma yellow. Style greenish. Filaments yellow. This is probably only a geographical form of *Echinopsis aurea*. My plants originate from Friedrich Ritter's wild collected seed, distributed by Hildegard Winter in Germany in 1960.

Echinopsis calochlora

Like *E. calorubra*, this species was used as one of the parents in the production of the earliest Abbey Brook hybrids, e.g. *E.* 'Abbey Brook' ABCN 2189. *E. calochlora* is usually solitary, but slowly forms clumps with age. The flowers are large and white and the species originates from Bolivia and Brazil.

Echinopsis calorubra

This is an important species with multicoloured flowers. It was used in the production of my earliest hybrids e.g. E. 'Abbey Brook' ABCN 2189. It slowly forms clumps with age, it may take 30 years! Large flowers, variable in colour, often red with orange and magenta tinges. Both *E. calochlora* and *E. orozasana* are referable here and come from Bolivia.

Echinopsis calorubra GC918.07 North of Vallegrande, Bolivia 2000m
Photo G Charles ©

Echinopsis eyriesii

An attractive species which is widely cultivated for its attractive spineless plants and large white flowers with a hint of pink at the tips. Offsets freely from the base and forms large clumps with age. Stigma white. Style green. Filaments white. Highly scented. This species, like *E. multiplex* may be synonymous with *E. oxygona*.

Echinopsis 'Golden Dream'

Parents unknown.
An American hybrid hybridised and distributed by Howard E. Gates from his nursery in California. My original plant came from Churchman's nursery in Mansfield Woodhouse near Nottingham in the 1950s. It is an attractive spiny plant with large yellow flowers. It probably has *E. aurea* in its parentage.

Echinopsis 'Green Gold'

Parents unknown
Deep golden yellow flowers. It is a dark green plant with few spines, freely offsetting from the base.
An American hybrid hybridised and distributed by Howard E. Gates from his nursery in California. My original plant came from Churchman's nursery in Mansfield Woodhouse near Nottingham in the 1950s. I have no idea what the parents might be. As Gordon Rowley (private communication) has suggested, the early American hybrids were randomly pollinated and the seedlings planted out in beds. After flowering, if any looked interesting, they were selected and propagated vegetatively.

Echinopsis hammerschmidii (n.b. not **hammerschmidtii**)

Originally described by Professor Cardenas. My plant came direct from him in the late 1950s collected at the type locality, Las Lajas in Bolivia. It is a clump forming plant with very large white flowers. It is named for a priest Father Hammerschmid who originally discovered it. In the 1990s I hybridised it with 'Brian's Choice' to produce a stunning new hybrid 'Darley Hammerschmid'.

Echinopsis kermesina

Closely related to *E. mamillosa*. It is smaller growing with yellow brown spines and has red magenta unscented flowers. These are tubular rather than open funnel-form. I have produced some very attractive hybrids using this species, namely E. 'Brian's Choice', × *Trichoechinopsis* 'Abbey Brook' and × *Trichoechinopsis* 'Ruth Fearn'. Late in 2007 I have managed to hybridise it with *Trichocereus fulvilanus*.

Echinopsis oxygona (better known as E. multiplex)

Plants with this name in cultivation appear very uniform, which is hardly surprising when its prolific production of offsets is considered. I am unsure whether it is a natural species or of horticultural origin. Nevertheless it produces very attractive pinkish white flowers, which are large, freely produced and highly scented. It is one of the parents of my own hybrid 'Darley Queen'.

Echinopsis orozasana FR 779

Originally discovered and collected by Friedrich Ritter at Orozas in Bolivia. Large white flowers which unusually open in full sunshine (white flowered species are usually nocturnal opening). It was described by Ritter as a variety of *E. mamillosa*, but it is probably closer to *E. calorubra*. I hybridised it over 30 years ago (CF3099) without noting the pollen donor. I cannot explain why one of the seedlings has yellow flowers. This has been named 'Sarah'.

Echinopsis 'Paramount Pink' *and* 'Paramount Yellow'

These are both Johnson's American hybrids of unknown parentage.
'Paramount Pink' has long-tubed bi-coloured flowers, inner petals white, outer petals pale magenta pink with a darker magenta midstripe. This hybrid is no improvement on either *E. eyriesii* or *E. multiplex*.
'Paramount Yellow' has long-tubed golden yellow flowers. The plants of both these hybrids are virtually spineless with small white felted areoles.

Echinopsis pereziensis

This species was originally discovered and described by Cardenas in 1963. It was found near Perez in Bolivia at 1900 metres.

I obtained this as a field collected plant from Hollygate Nursery in Sussex in 1973 on the occasion of the visit of the I.O.S. to the nursery during its Congress held at Reading. It produced very large wide-opening pure white flowers which were highly scented. I do not now have this species in cultivation. My first really successful cross was made between this species and *E. kermesina* in 1975. The resultant F_1 hybrid was named 'Brian's Choice'. All the first generation plants were identical, which confirms that the two parents were not of hybrid origin.

Echinopsis 'Red Meteor' and 'Terracotta'

These are included together as I have never cultivated either of them individually. In 1977 Margaret Martin, having heard of my work and interest in *Echinopsis* hybrids, sent me some seed of crosses she had made using these two cultivars. These I successfully grew and subsequently used the hybrid offspring to hybridise with some of my own hybrids to produce a new range of hybrids. These new hybrids must have very complex parentage.

At the same time Margaret sent me seed of other hybrid crosses including:

        CF2360 'Peach Monarch' × 'Tangerine'
        CF2361 'Peach Monarch' × 'Terracotta'
        CF2362 *E. coronata*
        CF2363 *E. kermesina* × *tamboensis*
        CF2364 'Green Gold' × 'Peach Monarch'
        CF2365 *E. multiplex* × collection
        CF2366 'Green Gold' × collection
        CF2367 *E. eyriesii* × 'Red Meteor'
        CF2368 'Green Gold' × 'Terracotta'
        CF2369 unknown parents

I selected and named, from several thousand seedlings raised from this seed, a few of the resulting offspring. To mark the contribution of Margaret's crosses to my work, I am looking for a suitable one of my new hybrids which will be named in her honour. As there is already an American hybrid named 'Margaret Martin', my hybrid will be named 'Margaret's Legacy'.

Echinopsis subdenudata

An attractive species which is spineless in age, and has large white felted areoles. It produces large pure white flowers.

According to *The New Cactus Lexicon* (Hunt 2006), *E. subdenudata*, originally described by Cardenas in 1956, is synonymous with *E. ancistrophora* as a spineless form. I am unsure as to the reasons for this, as *E. subdenudata* grows into a large multi-headed clump with age; whereas *E. ancistrophora* remains small and usually is solitary. The flowers are much smaller with the outer petals tinged pink.

Lobivia grandiflora

This is the name under which I have long grown this plant, although it is now called *Echinopsis rowleyi*. It is a most attractive plant, freely clumping from the base, but not growing over-large for the small greenhouse or conservatory. The flowers are spectacular, both in size, colour and production. The flowers are deep blood red with contrasting yellow stamens and stigma. 'Sir Joseph Paxton' and surprisingly 'Golden Wedding' are two new hybrids using this plant as a pollen donor.

Lobivia backebergii subsp. *schieliana*

This plant is now listed in *The New Cactus Lexicon* as *Echinopsis schieliana*. This name was originally applied by Curt Backeberg to plants reputedly collected by Friedrich Ritter (FR 334) and cultivated by Wolfgang Schiel in Germany. My plants have variable flower colours usually orange red but sometimes pale orange and deep red. There is also an attractive small form in cultivation called f. *pectinata* with adpressed pectinate spines and red flowers. I have recently hybridised subsp. *schieliana* with the salmon flowered hybrid of *E. arachnacantha*. See Fearn's Petite Hybrids in the Check List.

Lobivia purpureominiata

This plant is now listed in The New Cactus Lexicon as a synonym of Echinopsis huascha. The plants that I have long cultivated are significantly different. The black throat colour of the flowers is quite distinctive and the fewer stouter spines easily differentiate it from E. huascha.

It is another species with spectacular flowers which are purplish red with a black throat produced by the dark coloured stamens. I have recently been using it as a pollen donor to hybridise with some of my × Trichoechinopsis seedlings. 'Millennium' and 'Papa Dip' have so far been produced.

Also belonging here and closely related is Lobivia crassicaulis. This again is a plant I have long cultivated and which I am currently using as a pollen donor. Like Lobivia purpureominiata it has short-tubed, bell shaped flowers, deep orange red, but the throat on this plant is dark crimson. Stigma yellow, style reddish, filaments red. Scented.

Trichocereus fulvilanus

My plants have been grown from seed collected by Friedrich Ritter and described by him in 1962. This plant is possibly the same as T. deserticola described by Erich Werdermann in 1929. Tall growing spiny plants, with characteristic large orange felted areoles. The white flowers are, unusually, produced from the side of the plant. These are less than 10cm long, which is much smaller than in other members of the same genus. It originates from Chile. Gordon Foster has managed to hybridise it with an Echinopsis (probably E. eyriesii) and passed a cutting on to me. I have crossed Gordon's hybrid with 'Ruffles' in two further generations. 'Fulviruff' and 'Darley Oakdene' have been selected and named from these.

Trichocereus lamprochlorus

There is some confusion about which plant was originally described by Charles Lemaire in 1838. The plant that I have used is a stout, tall growing plant 8cm to 10cm in diameter with glossy green stems and gigantic white flowers. Its possible area of distribution is Bolivia. 'Sir Joseph Paxton' is one of its progeny in the second generation.

Trichocereus schickendantzii

This is a relatively short growing species that forms large multi-headed clumps. Huge funnel-form flowers are produced from the stem apex. These are pure white in colour and highly scented. It grows at Tucuman in north west Argentina. 'Garden News' is one of its hybrids.

Trichocereus thelegonus

Unlike other species, this one is prostrate and creeps along the ground with a raised stem apex. Most collectors try to grow it upright, but it needs firmly staking. The flowers are very large, funnel-form and pure white. Like *T. schickendantzii*, it comes from Tucuman in north west Argentina. One of my first hybrids was to cross this species with *E. kermesina*. It produced a spectacular result which was called × *Trichoechinopsis* 'Abbey Brook'. In the second generation, after further selection, another hybrid has been called 'Ruth Fearn'.

Bibliography

Abbey Brook Cactus Nursery (1977 – 2000) *Plant Lists*
Anderson, E.F. (2001) *The Cactus Family*. Timber Press, Portland, Oregon.
Backeberg, C. (1978) *Cactus Lexicon*. Blandford Press, Dorset, England.
Cullman, W. Götz, E., and Gröner, G. (1986) *The Encyclopedia of Cacti*. Alpha Books, Sherborne, Dorset, England.
Das, A.B. and Mohanty, S. (2006) Karyotype analysis and in-situ nuclear DNA content in seven species of *Echinopsis* Zucc. of the family Cactaceae. *Cytologia* **71** (1): pp.75 – 79
Fearn, B. (2002) Abbey Brook *Echinopsis* Hybrids – the results of 30 years' work. *Brit. Cact. Succ. J.* **20** (4): pp. 177 – 183
Friedrich, H. and Glaetzle, W. (1983) Seed morphology as an aid to classifying the genus *Echinopsis*. *Bradleya* **1**: pp. 91 – 104
Gröner, G. (2007) Hybriden der Kakteengattung *Trichocereus*. *Garten praxis* October 2007, pp. 56 – 61
Hunt, D., Taylor, N. and Charles, G. (2006) *The New Cactus Lexicon*. dh books, Milborne Port, England.
Meier, E. (1991) × *Aporophyllum* hort. *Kaktusblute* **8**: April
Preston – Mafham, R. and K. (1991) *Cacti – the illustrated dictionary*. Blandford Press, Dorset, England.
Rausch, W. (1975 – 6) *Lobivia: der tagblutigen Echinopsidinae aus areal*. Geographischer Sicht, 3 vols., Vienna.
Rippe, K. (1990) Die Schonheit der *Hildwintera* – Hybriden. *Kaktusblute* **7**: April
Rippe, K. (1991) *Pseudolobivia callichroma* – Hybriden. *Kaktusblute* **8**: April
Rowley, G.D. (1996) Worthwhile succulents. *Brit. Cact. Succ. J.* **21**: p. 82
Timmermans, A.J. (1984) Over de groei van cristaten: 1. *Succulenta* **63** (2): pp. 45 – 48
Taylor Marshall, W., and Woods, R.S. (1938) *Glossary of Succulent Plant Terms*. Abbey Garden Press.

Glossary

anther	the sac containing the pollen.
areole	the restricted area where the spines and/or flowers are borne.
BCSS	the British Cactus and Succulent Society.
Cactaceae	a family of succulent plants distinguished by seven characteristics |//
	1 Dicotyledonous – having two seed leaves
	2 Perennial – living for more than one year
	3 Fruit – a one-celled berry, without divisions
	4 Ovary of the flower below the insertion of the petals
	5 Having areoles or spine cushions
	6 Caulocarpic – not dying after flowering
	7 Having numerous stamens
caespitose	with several to many stems growing from a common base, forming low mounds.
chlorophyll	the green colouring matter of plants.
chlorotic	devoid of chlorophyll.
CITES	Convention on International Trade in Endangered Species of Wild Fauna and Flora.
clonotype	a propagule from the type specimen on which a species was based.
Echinopsis	a genus of South American cacti. Name from the Greek – having the appearance of a hedgehog.
F_1	symbol used for the first hybrid (filial) generation, i.e. the offspring of the hybridisation between plants of two different species etc.
F_2	symbol used for the second hybrid (filial) generation, i.e. the offspring of the hybridisation between F_1 plants.
F_3 to F_6	offspring of crosses between plants of the third to sixth generations.
filament	the stalk which carries the anther or pollen sac (see also stamen).
fimbriate	petals with fringed edges.
funnel-form	in a flower the tube gradually widens upwards.

IOS	International Organization for Succulent Plant Study.
Lobivia	a genus of cacti closely related to *Echinopsis* and *Trichocereus*. The name is an anagram of Bolivia.
nocturnal	refers to flowers that open after dark. These are usually scented and pollinated by moths or in some cases by bats.
nomenclature	the plant names of species, genera, tribes etc. which are in Latin, so that the same name may be intelligible to all nationalities.
spine	a pointed, more or less rigid structure arising from an areole. A spine is homologous with a modified leaf.
stamen	the male floral organ consisting of the anther and the filament.
sterile	a word applied to anthers that do not function, or of seeds which are unable to germinate.
stigma	the part of the flower that receives the pollen for the fertilisation of the ovule.
style	the stalk-like portion which connects the stigma with the ovary.
synonym	a surplus name applied to a genus or species which has already been validly named in accordance with the International Code of Botanical Nomenclature, or one used contrary to the rules of the Code so that it must be discarded.
Trichocereus	a genus of night flowering South American cacti, usually with large flowers and hairy flower areoles.
type	the specimen or specimens on which a species or subspecies is based. The type is usually deposited in a herbarium for reference of posterity.
type locality	the place where a type specimen was originally collected.

Index

Abbey Brook Cactus Nursery – 6
Accession Numbers – 14

CITES legislation, effects of – 6, 7
Cultivation –
    compost for – 12
    feeding – 12
    light and temperature – 12
    watering – 12

Darley Dale – 9

Echinopsis –
    ancistrophora – 86
    arachnacantha – 84, 87
    aurea – 87
    callochrysea – 88
    calochlora – 88
    calorubra – 89
    eyriesii, 89
    hammerschmidii – 90
    hybrids (suffix T =
    × *Trichoechinopsis* or
    × *Tricholobiviopsis* hybrids)
        'Abbey Brook' – 15
        'Abbey Brook'(T) – 73
        'Alice in Wonderland' – 15
        'Apple Blossom' – 16
        'Apricot Fancy' – 16
        'Ava' – 17
        'Ballet Dancers' – 18
        'Brian's 6X' – 10, 18
        'Brian's Choice' – 19
        'Brooklands' – 20
        'Buff Beauty' – 20
        'Buttercup' – 10, 21

'Buttermilk' – 21
'Cariba'(T) – 76
'Chatsworth'(T) – 74
'Chelsea Girl'(T) – 10, 75
'Chelsea Sunshine'(T) – 76
'Cleopatra' – 22
'Crimson Glow' – 23
'Crown of Gold' – 24
'Darley Ann' – 25
'Darley Apricot' – 25
'Darley Beauty' – 26
'Darley Gold' – 10, 27
'Darley Hammerschmid' – 26
'Darley Leopard' – 28
'Darley Lilac' – 28
'Darley Oakdene'(T) – 78
'Darley Peach' – 29
'Darley Pearl' – 29
'Darley Pinwheel' – 30
'Darley Queen' – 30, 84
'Darley Rose' – 31
'Darley Sunbeam' – 31
'Darley Sunrise' – 32
'Darley Sunset' – 33
'Delicate' – 33
'Derbyshire Sunset' – 10, 34
'Eleanor' – 36
'Electric' – 35
Fearn's Petite Hybrids – 36
'Flamingo' – 37
'Fulviruff'(T) – 77
'Garden News'(T) – 78
'Gillian'(T) – 79
'Gilly's Favourite – 37

'Gold Star' – 39
'Golden Dream' – 84, 90
'Golden Eye' – 38
'Golden Fleece' – 39
'Golden Progress' – 40
'Golden Wedding'(T) – 10, 79
'Goldie' – 10, 40
'Green Gold' – 84, 90
'Green Ice' – 41
'Harlequin' (T) – 80
'Janet' – 41
'Jennifer Ann' – 43
'Jo' – 42
Johnson's unnamed hybrid – 84, 85
'Juliette' – 43
'King Midas' – 44
'Lemon Custard' – 45
'Lemonade' – 46, 84
'Les Parkin' – 80
'Lisa' – 46
'Loganberry Pete'(T) – 81
'Lotus Blossom' – 47
'Lyndsey' – 47
'Margot Fonteyn' – 48
'Marie' – 48
'Matlock Gem' – 49
'Matlock Sunset' – 49
'Millennium'(T) – 81
'My Rosalie' – 50
'Mystic Moon' – 50
'Orange Blossom' – 51
'Orange Garden' – 51
'Orange Ice Cream' – 52
'Orange Queen' – 52
'Orange Sensation' – 53

'Papa Dip'(T) – 82
'Paramount Pink' – 91
'Paramount Yellow' – 91
'Party Frock' – 53
'Peach Monarch' – 84
'Peach Sundae' – 54
'Pineapple Poll' – 54
'Pink Camay' – 55
'Pink Champagne' – 55
'Pink Glory' – 56
'Pink Nymph' – 56
'Primrose Beauty' – 57
'Princess Diana' – 57
'Princess Margaret' – 58
'Raspberry Ripple'(T) – 82
'Raspberry Sorbet' – 59
'Really Pretty' – 59
'Red Meteor' – 92
'Ruffles' – 10, 60, 84
'Rufflette' – 61
'Ruth Fearn'(T) – 83
'Sangria' – 62
'Sarah' – 62
'Sheryl' – 63
'Shirley' – 63
'Sir Joseph Paxton'(T) – 83
'Shot Silk' – 64
'Son of Orange Sensation' – 64
'Starlight' – 65
'Starlight Express' – 65
'Sterling Silver' – 66
'Streaky' – 67
'Summer Carnival' – 68
'Summer Glory' – 68
'Sunny Jim' – 66
'Susan' – 69

    'Swan Lake' – 69
    'Tango' – 70
    'Terracotta' – 84, 92
    'Titania' – 70
    'Turkish Delight' – 71
    'Van Gogh' – 72
    'Wedding Silk' – 72
  kermesina – 84, 90
  oxygona (*multiplex*) – 91
  orozasana – 91
  pereziensis – 92
  subdenudata – 93

Lobivia –
  backebergii subsp. *schieliana* – 93
  grandiflora – 93
  purpureominiata – 94

Pests, mealy bug and control – 13

Seed, germination percentage – 11
Seed, stock numbers – 14

Trichocereus –
  fulvilanus – 94
  lamprochlorus – 95
  schickendantzii – 95
  thelegonus – 95

BRIAN FEARN has been fascinated with cacti and succulents for over 60 years. He founded Abbey Brook Cactus Nursery in 1956 and has been raising Echinopsis hybrids since the 1960s. In this booklet he describes the story of this work and the 130+ beautiful hybrids he has selected and named out of the 150,000 seedlings that he has flowered.